PRISCILLA
Smocking
Book

Published by
The Priscilla Publishing Co
Boston Mass

The
Priscilla Smocking Book

A COLLECTION OF BEAUTIFUL
AND USEFUL PATTERNS

WITH

Directions for Working

BY

LOUISE FLYNN

PRICE, 25 CENTS

PUBLISHED BY

The Priscilla Publishing Company

85 BROAD STREET, BOSTON, MASS.

A Charming Party Dress for a Little Girl, Which Shows the Use of Smocking in Its Simplest Form. See Fig. 55

THE ART OF SMOCKING

SMOCKING is not new, but is a form of needle-work which is always in demand because of its simplicity and beauty, and the opportunity it affords for originality of design. It is, in a few words, the embroidery of simple stitches upon the folds or plaits of a shirred foundation, and may be used on any garment where fullness is desirable. It is charming for children's dresses, coats, bonnets, and muffs, as well as women's waists, dresses, smocks, and other articles of wearing apparel. The garments and simple designs shown in this book should arouse an added interest in this original, almost freehand work, in which designs may be created as the work progresses.

Materials.—The materials which may be used are most varied, including linens, crêpes, all silks not too thin, striped and checked dimities, lawns, ginghams, and similar goods, as well as velvet, chiffon, lace, albatross, cashmere, and other woolen fabrics of like character. On silk or woolen materials, silk threads should always be used for smocking, and on cotton fabrics, embroidery cotton either fine or coarse, depending upon whether a fine or coarse effect is desired. Two threads of stranded cotton are perhaps the best for work upon children's frocks and ladies' blouses when delicate shading and elaborate stitchery are to be accomplished. For more simple work in one color on gingham or crêpe, a heavier embroidery cotton may be used.

Preparation of Material. — As has already been stated, smocking is embroidery upon the folds or plaits of a shirred foundation material, and it is absolutely essential that this foundation be carefully prepared. In fact the most important thing in regard to smocking is the evenness of the gathering. This cannot be too strongly impressed, as the whole beauty of the work depends upon it. Various methods have been em-

FIG. 1. GATHERING THREADS IN PROCESS ON A CHECKED MATERIAL. See page 3

ployed at different times by different workers in arranging a guide for the placement of these gathering threads, the object being to space the threads at even distances apart and to place the gathering stitches in each row directly under those in the one preceding, taking up the same amount of material in each stitch.

Checked and Striped Materials.—Perhaps the simplest way of arriving at this result and one ideal for the beginner in smocking is the use of checked and striped materials, as in Figs. 1, 2, and 3 on this page.

Figure 1 shows perfectly the method for preparing a piece of checked dimity for smocking stitches. In this case the first and third lines are taken up for shirring, and two checks are omitted. This distance between stitches would make coarse work, about four or four and one-half times for fullness when finished, depending on the size of your check.

FIG. 2. GATHERING THREADS IN PROCESS ON A STRIPED MATERIAL WITH LINES MARKED BY MACHINE STITCHING. See page 3

Figure 2 shows the use of a material with a stripe, like striped dimity, that can be used for length of stitch. Here we first show lines stitched by using the sewing-machine, the width between the lines being regulated by the presser foot. This little device of stitching the lines is of the greatest value in using striped materials, especially the striped dimity, where the cords space the stitches. The stitching serves only as a guide for the gathering threads, and is clipped bit by bit and removed as the gathering threads are run in. If the cords are too far apart, one stitch between can be used; if the cords are too close together, one can be omitted. Thus it is readily seen

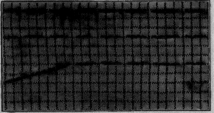

FIG. 3. A FINE CHECKED MATERIAL MAY ALSO BE USED. See page 4

3

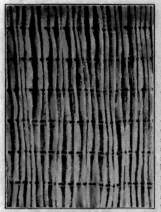

FIG. 4. CHECKED MATERIAL AS IN FIG. 1, WITH GATHERING THREADS. See page 4

either fine work or the reverse is easily attainable and can be correctly prepared.

Figure 3. — Here again is s h o w n a checked material fine enough for every other c h e c k to be omitted in the s h i r r i n g, as shown, and the same distance left between the rows of shirring, making a square. After these samples have been shirred, t h e threads drawn up moderately snug and securely tied in pairs, the pieces are ready for the smocking stitches.

Each line of gathering must have a separate thread, and each thread should be started at the right-hand side with a double stitch to hold the knot so that it will not slip through when the thread is drawn up. In this illustration a coarse cotton has been use l for gathering in order to show clearly, but a stout sewing cotton is all that is necessary.

Figure 4.—This illustration shows Fig. 1 with the gathering threads drawn up. It is the wrong side of the work. The right side, upon which the smocking stitches are worked, presents a succession of folds. (See Fig. 9.)

The Sewing-Machine Method.—As before stated, it is of the greatest importance in smocking that the work is perfectly prepared, as the entire beauty of the work would be marred by imperfect lines in the shirring. To attain this perfection on plain material the sewing-machine may be used for marking lines

and spaces. The lines are to work upon and the spaces are the size of the stitch, the presser foot being the guide between the lines. (See Fig. 5.) When the rows of stitching are complete, the threads are clipped about every two inches and removed a few at a time in a manner not to obliterate the impression made by the machine-needle. These marks or holes are used to determine the length of the shirring stitch, as you shir in the holes the machine-needle has made. If very fine work is desired, adjust the machine to eight stitches to the inch. This gives you a fullness of three times and is suitable for fine material. For heavier material adjust the machine to six stitches to the inch. This gives about four times the fullness. Smocking should rarely be fuller than this and is seldom used with less fullness than twice and one-half, which is very fine work. In using the stitched lines, the presser foot gives you the width, the size of the stitch gives you the length of your stitch for smocking.

Table for Fullness. — 4 times the material for fullness—six machine stitches to the inch.

FIG. 5. LINES AND SPACES MARKED BY SEWING MACHINE. FIRST SHIRRING THREAD BEING RUN. See page 4

3 times the fullness—eight machine stitches to the inch.

2½ times the fullness—ten machine stitches to the inch.

Figure 5 shows the lines of machine-stitching with first shirring thread in process. A study of the principle involved discloses the various possibilities the method opens up for the work. With the exception of some honeycomb designs and the foregoing elemental studies in checks, all of the work shown

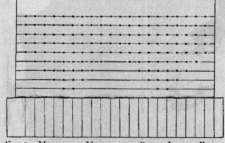

FIG. 7. METHOD OF MARKING BY RULED LETTER PAPER. See page 5

FIG. 6. MATERIAL MARKED WITH TRANSFER DOTS. See page 5

4

in this book was done using this simple method of the stitched lines. Indeed the writer has yet to use any other method than this. On your sewing-machine adjust the length of stitch according to the requirements of the work, either long for coarse or short for fine work. Let the presser foot guide the spaces, and you can mark up your material correctly and quickly.

Using this method is the only possible way to smock on curves correctly. (See Fig. 33 on pages 16 and 17.) A perfect circle ten inches in diameter was used for the yoke shown. The entire piece of work was stitched row after row, using the presser foot of the machine to guide the distance between the lines. One can readily grasp the principle of evenness of smocking, and unless the machine used is at fault, the work must be correct. Crease a line or mark with a thread just where the first stitch begins for each succeeding row of stitching.

Fig. 9. Outline Stitch in Process, and Some Variations. See page 5

Figure 6. Shirring by Means of Dots. — This illustration shows an example of the dotted lines as used in the preparation of material for smocking. This dotting can be accomplished with the transfer patterns which are prepared for the purpose; or by the method described and illustrated in Fig. 7. It is useful for velvet, as the sewing-machine injures or marks the pile of the velvet. The method is good to use also for a fabric like chiffon, which does not stitch well unless a paper is placed below it, as one works on lace. Mark the dots on the wrong side of the material, and in shirring take up the dots the same way as the cords of the checked dimity. (See Fig. 1 and pattern of dots on page 32.)

Figure 7. — Another method of marking material with dots is accomplished with two sheets of ruled letter paper and impression paper. Place the material to be dotted over the impression paper and the lined paper above this, one sheet with the lines perpendicular and one sheet with the lines horizontal. Now with a pencil, or other not too sharp point, dot out your dotted lines or points as you wish, mov-

Fig. 8. Outline Stitch. See page 5

ing the perpendicular lines down from the horizontal lines from line to line. For a small piece of work this is practical and is at every woman's command. Enough preparation for a child's dress can be done correctly in a few minutes' time without the use of a sewing-machine or any outside assistance such as transfers.

Smocking Stitches

Figure 8. Outline Stitch. — This stitch is most simple. It is in fact the well-known embroidery stitch worked from left to right on the plaits of the shirred material, the gathering thread acting as a guide to keep the work straight. It is used in starting most pieces of smocking.

Start your thread on the second plait at the gathering thread on the wrong side of the material, bringing the needle up in the first plait on the right side of the material. Take one stitch from left to right in the top of each plait, keeping the thread below the needle, and each stitch directly over the gathering thread. Fasten off thread at end of each row. This illustration shows four rows of outline stitch worked on material dotted and shirred as in Fig. 6.

Figure 9. Outline Stitch Variations. — Here we have plain material with rows of smocking worked in various examples of the outline stitch. The preparation for the work was the stitched lines described in Fig. 5, the goods shirred, threads secured, and the material gently pulled into position as seen. Then on the first row of shirring was worked one row of outline stitch across the line as shown. The second row was done in the same manner and third is in process, position of the needle showing exactly how the stitch is taken. The fourth row shows two rows of outline worked close together; the first worked on the line as previously; the second row below the first and close to it. The fifth row shows four rows in out-

Fig. 10. Double Outline Stitch. See page 6

5

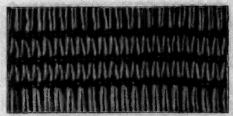

FIG. 11. SINGLE CABLE STITCH. See page 6

line and forms a band. When using shades of one color this simple border becomes quite elaborate and can be worked thus: The first row with the thread kept below the needle; the second row with the thread kept above the needle; the third row, as the first row, with the thread kept below the needle; the fourth row with the thread above the needle.

Figure 10. Double Outline Stitch. — The braided effect shown by this sample is secured by working two rows of outline stitch closely together over each gathering thread; in one row the thread being held above the needle, and in the other below the needle.

Figure 11. Single Cable Stitch. — This stitch is worked from left to right and is very much like the outline stitch. You start your thread at the gathering thread on the wrong side of the material, securing your knot in the second plait, and bringing the needle up in the first plait on the right side of the material as in outline stitch. Take one stitch in every plait, keeping the thread above the needle in the first stitch and below the needle in the next stitch, then above the needle again, and so on to the end of the line, keeping each stitch exactly on top of the gathering thread.

Figure 12. Double Cable Stitch. — This stitch is in order at this time, but the beginner is advised to leave it until she has acquired some of the other stitches, as it may be somewhat confusing. The double cable stitch is simply two rows of single cable worked closely together, the first slightly above the gathering thread and the second slightly below. Work the first row as previously described (Fig. 11, Single Cable), and in the second row reverse the order of the thread above or below the needle. As the first row begins with the thread above the needle, the second should begin with the thread below the needle. These

three lines of double cable, if worked in colors, are sufficient decoration for a child's play dress of blue chambray or natural-color linen. On blue the colors could be Turkey-red first row; a blue different from the dress, second row; and one shade of orange. On natural-color linen dark brown, orange, and black with a touch of green would be most effective. Thus, at an expense of a few cents, an otherwise plain unattractive play frock is made a thing of beauty and a joy to the small wearer.

Figure 13. Single and Double Wave Stitch. — The wave proper consists of four stitches worked gradually up and four stitches worked gradually down again in the outline stitch, and is worked from

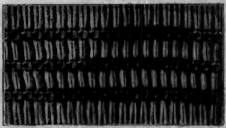

FIG. 12. DOUBLE CABLE STITCH. See page 6

left to right. Start your thread on the second plait on the right side of material as in outline, and work to the line above, using one, two, three stitches, one in each plait with the thread below the needle going up. Now with the thread above the needle take one stitch on the line next to the third stitch up with the thread above the needle and work to the line below, using three stitches gradually. Then with the thread below the needle take one stitch next to the last stitch on the line and work again to the line above, using three stitches and repeat. If your space permits you can use four stitches in place of three, and sometimes five or six stitches, using two lines. This depends on the pleasure of the worker and the result to be attained. Two or more rows of wave stitch may be worked one above the other as in the illustration.

Figure 14. — Double cable stitch repeated in many rows is extremely effective, especially when the work is done in shades of one color. Double Cable when used in this manner is most exacting, and no mistakes can possibly be

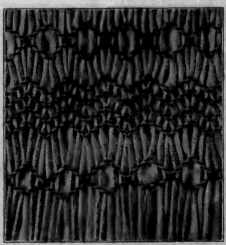

FIG. 13. SINGLE AND DOUBLE WAVE STITCH. See page 6

permitted, as one false stitch throws all into confusion. This pattern is particularly good for a boy's frock. The top and bottom rows may be black and those between in color.

A Double Wave or Diamond Wave is worked in the same manner as the single wave, working the sec-

FIG. 14. A SECOND EXAMPLE OF DOUBLE CABLE STITCH.
See page 6

ond row of wave in the opposite direction from the first rows, forming a diamond pattern as shown at top and bottom of Fig. 13.

This pattern used on a girl's simple play or school frock would be charmingly distinctive if the material was in pink and white stripe, either lawn, dimity or madras, the stripes about one-eighth of an inch wide. After stitching the lines on your sewing-machine, gather for the work, taking up the white lines and putting the pink lines in the background. This gives a white space for smocking, which can be done to advantage, using four shades of pink cotton, size 5. Stitch about twelve rows for this pattern. On the third row from the top line the double wave or diamond shown in the design is worked. This design is good and more important-looking if four stitches are used up and four down for the diamond.

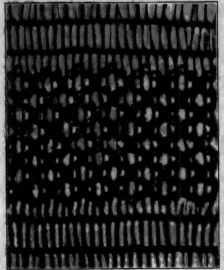

FIG. 16. FEATHERED DIAMOND STITCH WITH DOUBLE ROWS OF OUTLINE TOP AND BOTTOM. See page 8

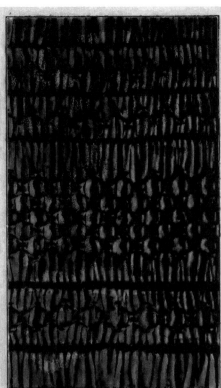

FIG. 15. DIAMOND STITCH COMBINED WITH SINGLE AND DOUBLE OUTLINE, FIGS. 8 AND 10. See page 8

Practice a little and determine which way you like the best. The second row of the diamond is commenced on the fourth line and worked up to meet the intersection of the diamond on the line above, forming a complete diamond. By close study of the illustration it is made very clear how this is worked. On the sixth line the single wave is commenced. Securing the thread and starting as for the diamond stitch, work from the sixth line to the fifth line the same number of stitches as in the diamond above, making the same turn on the line, two stitches, one up and one down, as in the diamond. Work as many rows as you are using shades of a color, and finish with the same diamond used to begin the design.

The work on the sleeve could be simplified using one row of diamond, two rows of wave, one row of diamond; or simply one row of diamond is good here, with a row of outline stitch each side of it. It is safe to allow three and one-half times for fullness used to smock in this manner.

A Curved Wave (see Fig. 10) is worked from line

of any gathering thread to the line above, using four stitches, as in single wave; then three stitches on the line; then four stitches down to the line below; then three stitches on this line; then four stitches up to the line above; and as before, three stitches on the line. It is important to remember that in going up in all forms of the wave the thread is kept above the needle. Very little practice, and one acquires this quite readily. The necessity of some practice is urged upon the learner, before attempting garments. The curved wave is usually used double, the second row the same as the first, one line apart, as in Fig. 10.

Figure 15. Diamond Stitch. — The stitch is worked from left to right. Start your thread as in previous directions. Take one stitch in the first plait over the gathering thread, with your thread below the needle, then one stitch in the second plait beside the first stitch, with the thread above the needle. This is the same as the cable stitch. Next pass down to half-way between the first and second gathering thread, and take one stitch in the third plait with the thread above the needle, and another stitch in the fourth plait beside the third with the thread below the needle. Then pass up again to the first gathering thread and take one stitch in the fifth plait with the thread below the needle, and the stitch beside it in the sixth plait with the thread above the needle; and continue to the end of the line. Be careful to take one stitch in every plait. This gives one-half of the diamond. The other half of the diamond is formed by starting on the second gathering thread and working up to half-way between the second and first gathering thread, so that the stitches meet the first half of the diamond.

This simple pattern looks well when worked on the cotton crêpes so much in favor for lingerie and simi-

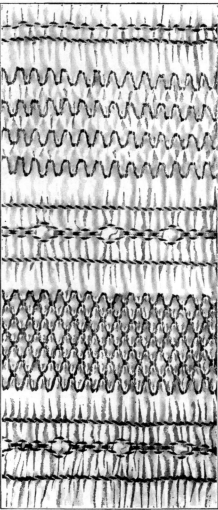

Fig. 17. Single and Double Vandyke Stitch Combined with Outline (Fig. 8), Cable (Fig. 11), and Wave (Fig. 13)

lar uses. After marking the shirring lines on the sewing-machine shir the material, using the holes made by the machine-needle in stitching the rows. A fullness of three times is desirable. On the first gathering thread work outline stitch, then one row of one-half diamond; then outline; then comes one-half diamond on the fourth row; then outline again on the fifth row, thus finishing the top of the pattern. On the seventh shirring thread begin the diamond stitch that forms the centre band, using three stitches up and three stitches down the one-half diamond. Work six rows, making five complete diamonds. If you wish a wider band do more rows, of course. Shades of blue may be used throughout. The double outline is used, as shown in the bottom row, with diamond stitch between. A wise selection of materials and perfect workmanship makes these simple patterns charming.

The lower band consisting of one row of diamond stitch with outline on either side is all that is needed for the sleeves.

Figure 16. Feathered Diamond.—We here have one of the most desirable stitches used in smocking, the feathered diamond. In appearance it is most elaborate, and it lends itself especially to shaded work and where a solid elaborate effect is desired. All workers are enthusiastic over the possibilities of the feathered diamond, and in the working it grows rapidly, presenting few difficulties. It is really one of the easiest stitches to acquire and one of the most agreeable to make. This sample was worked in navy blue cotton No. 5 on white linen; eighteen rows of stitching were required for the gathering threads. The first and third rows of smocking are in outline with feathered diamond commenced on the fourth row of shirring at the right. It is to be remembered that the feathered diamond is one of three stitches that is worked from right to left.

8

You begin by securing the thread on the second plait as usual, that the knot does not get loose and spoil the work. Bring the needle up on the first plait on the right side of the goods on the first gathering thread. Now take the first and second plaits together, keeping the thread before the needle as in ordinary feather stitch; then one-half way between the first and second gathering thread take the second and third plaits together; then just escaping the second gathering thread take the third, and fourth plaits together; the thread as previously used before the needle. Then up to one-half way between the first and second gathering thread take the fourth and fifth plaits together; then on the first gathering thread take the fifth and sixth plaits together; then down half-way between the first and second gathering thread take the sixth and seventh plaits together; and continue in this manner to the end of the line. This is one-half of a feathered diamond. The second row is worked similarly, starting on the third gathering thread and working to meet the first half diamond on the second gathering thread. Work until you have eight rows of diamonds. Finish as in the beginning with two rows in outline.

Figure 17. Vandyke Stitch. — This stitch is of unusual beauty and importance and is one of the few stitches worked from right to left. Start your thread

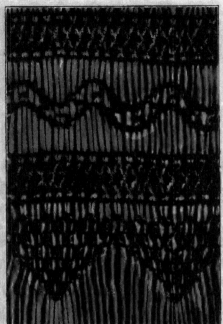

FIG. 19. THE CURVED WAVE IS HERE SHOWN, AND ANOTHER VARIATION OF THE DIAMOND POINT. See page 12

on the second plait on the right-hand side of the material in the usual manner on the first gathering thread. Bring the needle up on the first plait on the right side of the material. Pass the needle through the first two plaits together, and take one over. Then come down to the second gathering thread and take the second and third plait together with another stitch over. Then up again taking the third and fourth plait together with another stitch over; and so on to the end of the line. If the space between the lines is wide enough, as when the shirring is done by the transfer dot method, you can start half-way between the two gathering threads and work down or up to the lines. A space of half the distance between two gathering threads should always be left after every line of this stitch when worked single.

The Double Vandyke Stitch is simply two rows of single Vandyke stitch. Start your thread on the third gathering thread, working up to the second gathering thread; then down to the third gathering thread, according to the previous directions given for the single Vandyke.

The Vandyke and the double Vandyke are used to advantage in points where either 'stitch has been used in connection with the pattern above the point (See Figs. 26 and 28). The single Vandyke is at its

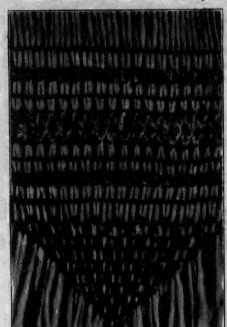

FIG. 18. POINT WORKED IN DIAMOND STITCH ON CHECKED DIMITY. See page 11

FIG. 20. BLOUSE OF CHECKED DIMITY SMOCKED IN BLUE. See Detail Fig. 22 and page 13

best when in a point. One-half a line or space is kept open between rows of single Vandyke, as shown. The double Vandyke is used to good advantage to finish a pattern, giving a fringe-like effect; it can be used where the Vandyke has been used in the pattern above it. Be careful to separate different stitches or patterns by a row of outline or cable stitch; otherwise, the beauty of the stitches is lost and a confused effect is the result.

There are only four stitches used in smocking that are worked from right to left: the Feathered Diamond; the Vandyke; the little embroidered dot that is frequently worked between lines; also the Honeycomb stitch.

The illustration (Fig. 17) begins with a row of single cable, which is really outline stitch with the thread reversed every other stitch. First the thread is below the needle; then above the needle; then below the needle; then above the needle. This row of single cable is followed by a row in single outline. The useful and attractive band separating the single Vandyke from the double Vandyke is placed between two rows of single outline, and is composed of stitches in double cable; then a full diamond worked, using three stitches up and three stitches down. Then two double cable stitches followed by the diamond stitch, and these stitches are alter-

FIG. 21. FAGOT-ING STITCH. See page 13

nated across the line. Nothing is better than this simple line of stitches where an inconspicuous separating line is desired. This illustration was worked on a striped dimity, lines stitched and spaces for stitches for shirring gauged by lines in the dimity.

The student in smocking who has mastered all of the preceding studies or illustrations, may now have the satisfaction of being rewarded, as we are ready for work on every variety of garment permitting the use of smocking. For blouses, handkerchief linen, crêpe, chiffon cloth, etc., are favorite materials. Garden and sports smocks are being reproduced for house wear in Italian silk and crêpe de Chine, voiles and other lovely materials. All sorts of lingerie are worked appropriately in this mode, and boudoir caps, matinées, etc., are included in the list. Motor bonnets are seen smocked to advantage. In children's wear frocks come first, and are made from six months' size to the party frock for a miss of fourteen years with equally satisfactory results. A lovely crêpe for the house smocks comes in part wool and part silk at a moderate price, and when showing a dainty flower or dot of color, the smocking may be in the same colors with fine effect. A wider field for originality is seldom open to an investigating mind.

FIG. 22. DETAIL OF SMOCKING ON BLOUSE, FIG. 20

Figure 18. The Making of Points. — Checked dimity was used for speed in working. Eleven rows of shirring was used. This includes only two rows of diamond in the point to be shirred. The new idea in this illustration is the point in diamond stitch. If the preceding studies and illustrations have been assimilated the worker is ready for the point, which is made without shirring its full depth. A most important time-saving demonstration, which the worker is urged to acquire.

One goes readily through the body of the design, using first outline stitch, then double cable, then outline in position shown, then our recent lesson in Vandyke is put into practice; then outline and double cable and outline again finish the body of the design; and here we encounter our point on the second row below the outline. The first row of diamond is worked from line to line above across the line. The second row is worked in the same manner as the first row except you begin on the third row of shir-

FIG. 23. BULLION STITCH
See page 13

FIG. 24. REVERSE OVER-AND-OVER STITCH. See page 13

ring and work to the second row to meet the first row of diamond. (See Fig. 15.) This makes, as you see, a perfect diamond.

Now holding your work so that the plaits are perpendicular as shown, work the second diamond, dropping one-half diamond on each side, or making each succeeding row one diamond less than the preceding one. As the eye is now trained to distance and one knows the requirements, it is unnecessary to shir for the point. Hold the work as directed, or secure the top of the piece to a table or other firm surface, using thumbtacks and holding each fold where it would naturally be if shirred. Pull the plaits in place. It is advisable to baste or sew firmly a piece of cloth across the top of your work to use in pinning it down with the thumbtacks. In this way your smocking is not injured, and you can hold your plaits as tightly as is necessary. One might, if experiencing difficulties, practice a point by itself.

11

dots are worked from right to left. Two plaits are taken together and two stitches taken over them. Then the needle is carried under two plaits, and in the next two plaits another dot is worked. The point in this case begins with one row of full diamond across the piece. This row of diamonds is divided into spaces of six diamonds. As one proceeds drop one diamond in every succeeding row, one-half on either side. These two patterns are charming and quite elaborate enough for all ordinary uses. Of course, if you *fail* to make *your point* without shirring, you will have to resort to shirred lines until you are a more independent worker.

Spacing Points. — There is no inflexible rule for spacing points, as points are used large or small, as suits the requirements of the work and the taste of the worker. (See Figs. 18 and 19.) Count your diamonds when across the line. Divide the number evenly if you can, or unevenly, if you must. Make as many points as required, using the same number of stitches in all. If you have twenty-five diamonds you can have five points of four diamonds each, leaving always a space between the points of one diamond in the first row. As rows increase the space increases in proportion, as you drop one-half diamond on either side as you proceed or narrow your work. Suppose you find you have twenty-five diamonds in all; you must start four points of four diamonds each, making twenty diamonds. Now you have one extra diamond to provide for and can use

FIG. 25. POINT IN DIAMOND STITCH. See Fig. 15 and page 14

Figure 19 is again worked on checked dimity to further illustrate the point. The outline and Vandyke stitch are now old acquaintances, so we proceed to the curved wave. This is much admired, and gives an elaborate, unusual appearance to a piece of work. However, it is simple enough in execution. The wave we have had and mastered (Fig. 13), and the curved wave is very similar. Thus work from a given line four outline stitches up to the line above; then, curving very slightly, three stitches in outline are worked just above the line; then four outline stitches are worked down again to the first line; then three outline stitches are worked just below this line, and then four stitches in outline again to the line above; then the three in outline just above the line. This is one row of the curved wave. The second line is worked one space either below or above the first line. In this case, Fig. 10, fifteen lines were used or fifteen checks. The two rows of Vandyke were worked and then the curved lines or wave put. Between these lines is shown a row of dots in a deeper shade than the waved lines. These

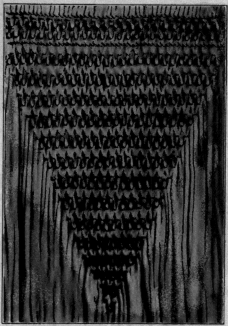

FIG. 26. POINT IN VANDYKE STITCH. See Fig. 17 and page 15

this in the centre or third point to advantage, as it usually looks better to have the centre of the garment with a deeper point than the other points. The illustration shows a point of nine diamonds. Figure 19 shows a point of six diamonds, and one readily understands that points are not arbitrary factors, but are quite adaptable.

Figure 20. Ladies' Blouse of Checked Dimity. — The blouse shown is smocked and embroidered in three shades of blue. Two threads of stranded cotton were used throughout.

Waist and sleeves are of the checked dimity, with collar, cuffs, and vestee of handkerchief linen edged with applied hems of the dimity.

The materials used were as follows: Three yards checked dimity; 5 skeins stranded cotton; 1 dozen buttons; ½ yard handkerchief linen, for collar, vestee, and cuffs. The applied hems were finished on their edges with a reversed over-and-over stitch (see Fig. 24), and joined to collar, cuffs, and vestee, using the fagoting stitch with buttonhole stitch down the centre, as shown by Fig. 21. The illustration does not convey an adequate impression of the charming color and stitch combinations. A useful finish having very good effect was the simulated buttons or spiders on either side of the blouse front worked in two shades of blue. (See Fig. 51, page 26.) No detailed description is needed of these stitches, as the illustrations are perfectly comprehensive. To make the sprays of embroidery a spool is

Fig. 27. JABOT SHOWING A PRACTICAL APPLICATION OF POINT IN DIAMOND OR VANDYKE STITCH. See page 16

Fig. 28. POINT IN DOUBLE VANDYKE STITCH. See Fig. 17 and page 16

used to curve the stems that are marked with a pencil and worked in outline stitch. The budlike effect of the bullion-stitch embroidery is secured by taking three stitches in bullion stitch, winding the thread six times around the needle. (See Fig. 23.) The centre stitch can be in a deeper shade, with charming effect.

The smocking pattern across the top of the waist fronts where attached to the yoke is shown in detail on page 11. Any waist pattern may be used which provides for gathered fronts attached to a shoulder yoke, allowing for a fullness of three times, if checked dimity is used (as in Fig. 1). If plain material is used, and shirring threads marked by sewing-ma-

FIG. 29. HONEYCOMB SMOCKING DONE ON HAND-RUN TUCKS. See page 17

gun for the points, working to the sixteenth line six and one-half times across the line; the seventeenth line is worked to the sixteenth line, completing the diamond. Work across the line. (See detail of diamond stitch, Fig. 15.) The following rows of diamonds forming points are worked without shirring by holding or fastening the work in a manner to retain plaits already formed. This method possesses the added virtue of leaving the material free from shirring marks as well as being a time-saver. I never mark a point except when doing honeycomb work.

The finishing ornaments at the tip of the point are in bullion stitch taken three times, with the thread wound seven times around the needle. The needle used should be round eyed, as this sort has no enlargement at the eye and allows the stitch to slip easily off the needle. Otherwise the stitch is spoiled.

Figure 25. — The illustration shows a design suitable for women's frocks and blouses, or for children's frocks. When used on a crêpe de Chine frock or blouse the smocking stitches may be worked in silks of the same shade with a very good effect. The illustration shown was done with white cotton on plain pink madras. The sewing-machine was used to secure the lines and spaces, and in this case the point was also worked, using the shirred lines. Stitch

FIG. 29. HONEYCOMB SMOCKING DONE ON HAND-RUN TUCKS. See page 17

chine method, allow for fullness according to table on page 4. Beginners are advised to try a sample of the goods they wish to use for fullness, before beginning a blouse.

Figure 22. — This illustration shows in detail the work done on the blouse shown on the previous page, and a description of the stitches will not be given, reference to preceding directions being deemed sufficient. Nineteen rows of shirrings were made for the smocking of the fronts, using every second cord of the dimity, giving a fullness of three times. The first row is outline stitch; the second row double cable, which is two rows of single cable; the third row is outline; the fourth row is a curved wave, beginning on the fifth line and working to the fourth line; the fifth row is the second of the curved wave, beginning on the sixth line and worked to fifth line, four stitches up, one on each of four plaits, three above the line, and four stitches down to the line below (see illustration for proportions) just meets the line in the curve (see direction for curved wave, Fig. 19); the sixth line is outline; seventh line is double cable; eighth line is outline; ninth line is Vandyke worked down to the tenth line; tenth line just meets the line, leaving room for the lower Vandyke to join on the line; eleventh line, worked to the tenth line, is Vandyke, making double Vandyke; twelfth line is outline; thirteenth line is double cable; fourteenth line is outline. On the fifteenth line the diamond is be-

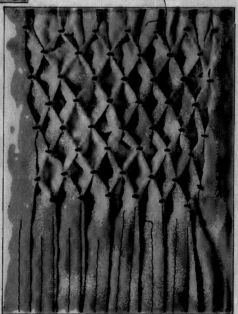

FIG. 30. MACHINE-STITCHED TUCKS ARE ALSO RECOMMENDED. See page 18

on your sewing-machine twenty-four lines.
Do the preparation for the smocking stitches
as shown by Fig. 5, page 4. Draw up the
shirring threads, secure them; pull the work
into place and work the first row in single
outline stitch (see Fig. 6, page 4). Work
the second row in single cable stitch across
the line (see Fig. 11); the third row in
single outline stitch across the line. On the
fourth gathering thread work a wave or
half-diamond, using three stitches up and
three stitches down (see Fig. 15), working
down to the fifth line. This gives one-half
of the diamond, as shown in the illustration.
(The wave and the half-diamond are frequently the same thing, depending on its
application.) The second row of diamond
stitch is worked, beginning on the sixth
gathering thread, and down to the seventh,
as shown by Fig. 15, page 7. Reversing the
points on the seventh gathering thread work
to the eighth, as on the line above. This
secures a wave effect on either side of a
diamond. This is often named the double
diamond.

This idea can be carried out in any number of stitches, thus increasing the size of
the wave and of the diamond, and several
rows of wave can be worked. When doing
shaded work this idea is extremely desirable. The three lines following this pattern
show single outline, cable and single outline, as in the beginning of the illustration.
Now we have a point worked in the diamond stitch, using two stitches, one up and
one down. Work one full diamond across

FIG. 31. CHILD'S LONG COAT OF WHITE FRENCH SERGE.
See page 18

the line; then divide the line, as is shown in the illustration. Work row after row in diamond stitch, dropping one-half diamond at each side of every row; thus
you narrow to a point. This is an excellent piece of
work for a beginner in smocking to practice on for
plain and shaded work, and to firmly establish the
principle of the point. In working the diamond point,
one applies the same principle as in the diamonds in
the centre of the middle row.

Figure 26.—Here we have the Vandyke stitch, both
single and double. The double Vandyke is shown in
one row of the band, with the familiar and useful
outline on either side. The single Vandyke forms the
point. The mastering of this illustration is most essential at this time, as used in connection with the previous illustration (Fig. 25). The detail of the Vandyke stitch is given on page 8, Fig. 17, and need not
be repeated here. This point, as shown, was worked
on striped dimity. The lines were stitched on the
sewing-machine and the cords in the material used

FIG. 32. DETAIL OF SMOCKING ON CHILD'S COAT

15

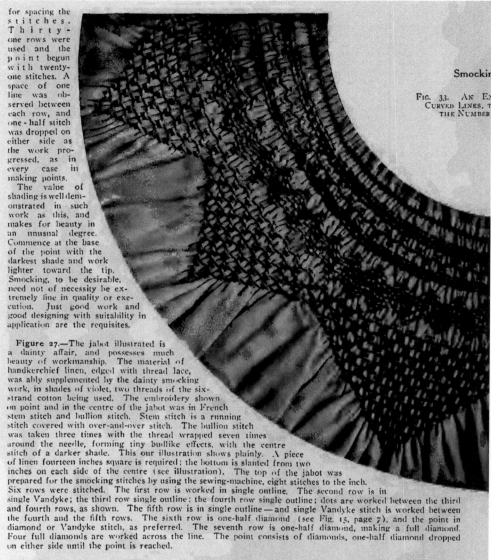

for spacing the stitches. Thirty-one rows were used and the point begun with twenty-one stitches. A space of one line was observed between each row, and one-half stitch was dropped on either side as the work progressed, as in every case in making points.

The value of shading is well demonstrated in such work as this, and makes for beauty in an unusual degree. Commence at the base of the point with the darkest shade and work lighter toward the tip. Smocking, to be desirable, need not of necessity be extremely fine in quality or execution. Just good work and good designing with suitability in application are the requisites.

Figure 27.—The jabot illustrated is a dainty affair, and possesses much beauty of workmanship. The material of handkerchief linen, edged with thread lace, was ably supplemented by the dainty smocking work, in shades of violet, two threads of the six-strand cotton being used. The embroidery shown on point and in the centre of the jabot was in French stem stitch and bullion stitch. Stem stitch is a running stitch covered with over-and-over stitch. The bullion stitch was taken three times with the thread wrapped seven times around the needle, forming tiny budlike effects, with the centre stitch of a darker shade. This our illustration shows plainly. A piece of linen fourteen inches square is required; the bottom is slanted from two inches on each side of the centre (see illustration). The top of the jabot was prepared for the smocking stitches by using the sewing-machine, eight stitches to the inch. Six rows were stitched. The first row is worked in single outline. The second row is in single Vandyke; the third row single outline; the fourth row single outline; dots are worked between the third and fourth rows, as shown. The fifth row is in single outline—and single Vandyke stitch is worked between the fourth and the fifth rows. The sixth row is one-half diamond (see Fig. 15, page 7), and the point in diamond or Vandyke stitch, as preferred. The seventh row is one-half diamond, making a full diamond. Four full diamonds are worked across the line. The point consists of diamonds, one-half diamond dropped on either side until the point is reached.

Figure 28.—Here we have a very important illustration, showing the Vandyke stitch in connection with the feathered diamond. Twenty-seven rows were prepared, using the sewing-machine for marking the lines and spaces. Six stitches to the inch gave the size of the plait. The work being prepared, on the first gathering thread work single outline; on the second and third gathering threads single Vandyke; third and fourth single Vandyke; the fifth row single outline. The fifth row shows outline again. The sixth, seventh, eighth, ninth, and tenth rows show feathered diamond to good advantage (see Fig. 16). The eleventh line is single outline, and now we have our point in double Vandyke, worked once across the line in full Vandyke and then divided

16

into points, as shown, of fourteen full Vandyke stitches.

Any number of stitches can be used that are liked. This stitch covers the work with a lacelike effect, and must not be worked too tightly. The stitch is not as elastic as others; but it is of great beauty, the richest point in smocking. Its slow execution deters workers from using it generally, yet the finest quality of work frequently shows this beautiful point.

Honeycomb Smocking.

—This is undoubtedly the first form of the smocking stitch, and is the stitch most frequently seen on women's dresses and coats, and to a considerable extent on children's garments. For a very handsome illustration, see Fig. 31.

There are several different methods of preparing material for honeycomb smocking, and all ways lead to the same result.

Material marked with dots, as Fig. 7, may be shirred or not, as preferred, for it is perfectly feasible to work the stitch on the dots without shirring.

Begin work on second row of dots at upper right-hand side. Fasten thread securely so that it will not pull through. Bring needle up through second dot, take first and second dots together, then over once again in first dot, pass needle up back of material to first row and take second and third dots together in same way. Down again to second row and take third and fourth dots together. Then to first and take fourth and fifth dots. In other words, the dot vertically parallel to the one last worked becomes the first in the succeeding stitch. A point begins with any number divisible by two or four and ends with two dots (see Fig. 7).

Figure 29.—This illustration shows a method of preparing material for the honeycomb stitch, which is at every woman's command — hand-run tucks run or basted into place. The tucks are measured as when doing any hand-tucking, the space between the tucks determining the size or width of the diamond. Use a card to measure for the length, which should be about the same as the width from point to point.

Honeycomb smocking done on tucked material is worked from the *left* side from top to bottom. Take first and second tucks together, over again, bring needle down inside second tuck to one-half the depth of the diamond, take second and third tucks together and one stitch over. Come down full length of diamond, take first and second tucks of diamond, take first and second tucks together as before, then second and third tucks again and repeat the length desired. One row of work gives two rows of dots. *2d row*—Take third and fourth tucks together, once over, come down one-half width of diamond and take fourth and fifth tucks together, and continue length desired. *3d row*—Take fifth and sixth tucks together, one-half diamond down take sixth and seventh tucks together, then fifth and sixth, and so on. The diamond should be oblong in shape when finished, although the material for each diamond is square.

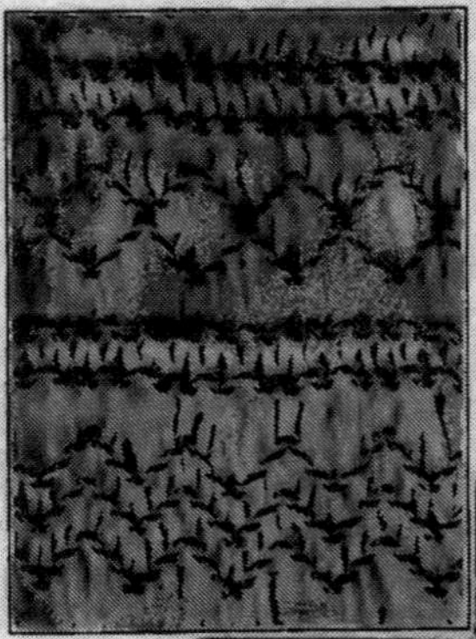

Figure 30 gives still another variation for preparing the honeycomb smocking. In this case the tucks were stitched on the sewing - machine, using the tucker for the purpose. This is recommended when an amount of smocking is to be made, as it is absolutely

which show the embroidered scallops matching the embroidery on the collars. Feather-stitching at the hems still further decorates this desirable coat for baby.

Figure 33.—To smock on any line except a perfectly straight one has not heretofore been accomplished; with the one exception of the Bishop model; and in that solitary case it has not been entirely successful. In this illustration is shown what can be accomplished on the curve when using the machine-stitched lines. You cannot possibly smock on a curve when using any other method. Heretofore patterns have conformed to their intended decoration when smocking was to be used, and the result has been a noticeable uniformity of outline in garments showing this em-

FIG. 34.
STITCHES
USED ON
SLEEVE OF
FIG. 35

right and works quickly. Here again one uses the card to measure the depth of the diamond. Use tucker as for all tucking, one - eighth-inch tuck, one - eighth-inch space, and so on.

Figure 31. — Here we show a practical application of honeycomb smocking. The work was done in this case on stitched lines. The points were stitched to the depth desired, and the smocking quickly done with great precision.

Figure 32 shows honeycomb smocking enlarged. The coat has a yoke, to which the smocking is joined, and the yoke is covered by the deep collar. The smocking is done on the back as on the front, and the upper collar is in two pieces, back and front alike.

The sleeves are smocked above the turn-up cuffs,

FIG. 35. CHILD'S BISHOP DRESS, SHOWING SMOCKING ON CURVED LINES. See Figs. 34 and 36, and page 19

bellishment, and but little progress has been made. With the advent of embroidered smocking, using the stitched lines, these conditions

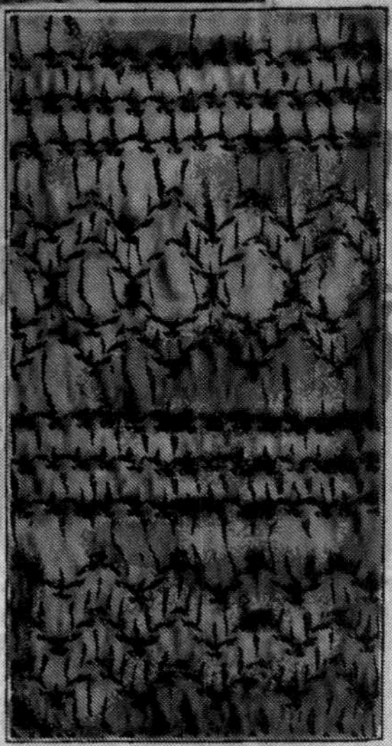

FIG. 36. STITCHES FOR YOKE OF FIG. 35

have been altered, and smocking has gained tremendously in popularity; as in using this method one can do smocking wherever one can stitch a line.

In preparing the material for the illustration, a perfect circle of ten inches in diameter was stitched on white sateen, using the sewing-machine for lines and spaces. Twelve rows were stitched, the circle widening to twenty inches, each successive row, of necessity, having many additional stitches and plaits, the last row doubling the first row. The points after the first two rows of diamonds were free-hand work or folds held in position from previous stitches. In smocking one is not likely to meet such a necessity as this; but the illustration is most useful as an example, and can be imitated in a modified form in many instances. The break in the stitches caused by the increasing number of plaits is handled, using outline stitch to divide the rows, thus permitting the use of the increased number of plaits. This is a piece of work much admired. It is unusual and a bit difficult. It is necessary in doing work like this that the material

FIG. 38. DETAIL OF SMOCKING ON CHILD'S DRESS, FIG. 37

FIG. 37. ANOTHER BISHOP DRESS, MADE OF CHECKED DIMITY AND SMOCKED IN SHADES OF PINK. See Fig. 38 and page 20

be well covered by the stitches, as unavoidably the folds or plaits are irregular. The stitches used are single outline on the first line, double cable on the second line, one-half diamond on the third line, and double cable on the fourth line. Following this are four lines of wave, using three stitches up and three stitches down for the wave. After these one row of full diamond, and then points made in diamond stitch. It will be noticed that the points vary in size; two points on either side begin with seven diamonds each, and two points in the centre of the work begin with ten diamonds each. The color used for working was navy blue, but shading would improve this or a similar pattern very much.

Figure 35. Child's Bishop Dress.— This practical and attractive little frock shows the Bishop or peasant model familiar to every mother. It is similar to our previous illustration in outline; and again the neck curve is pronounced and we apply the same principle in preparing the work, viz.: the stitched lines and spaces being used to fine advantage. The smocking

wave in three stitches. The edges of the collar and cuffs show the double over-and-over stitch (Fig. 24, page 11), and are further ornamented with little embroidered spiders (Fig. 51, page 26). This frock was also made worked in shades of red, and was more elaborate in appearance, owing to the shading. One makes a great mistake when one economizes on materials, as ordinary material greatly detracts from the best work, rendering it undesirable. It is better to err on the side of extravagance in material. The hand-made cord and tassels which lace together the collar points give a touch of distinction.

Figure 37. Child's Dress. — Here we have the Bishop model again in a different material and treatment. This little frock is in four-year-old size, and is very dainty. The material is cross-bar dimity, very fine, and the smocking is done in shades of rose-color.

Fig. 39. English Smock Model for Boy. See Figs. 40 and 41 and page 21

Fig. 40. Detail of Smocking on Back of Fig. 39

work on yoke, Fig. 36, consists of three rows of single cable, one row of wave in three stitches, one full diamond in three stitches, one row of wave in three stitches, three rows of single cable, three rows of wave as above. The smocking on the sleeve, Fig. 34, shows two rows single cable, one row full diamond, two rows single cable, and three rows of

This little frock has a Dutch neck and elbow sleeves; a four-inch hem, and a bit of ribbon-run lace heading at neck and sleeves completes the detail. Two yards of dimity and four skeins of cotton were the materials required for this little frock.

The illustration shows clearly the detail of the work on Fig. 37. The neck curves, and was therefore stitched for lines and spaces. Twelve lines were required, as the points were made free-hand. The first row was single cable; the second row, one-half diamond; the

Fig. 41. Detail of Smocking on Front of Fig. 39

Fig. 42. Blouse of Fine Checked French Dimity Smocked and Embroidered in Shades of Blue. See detail, Fig. 43, and page 21

third row, single cable; the fourth row, dots; the fifth row, single cable; the sixth, seventh, and eighth rows wave in three stitches; the ninth row, single outline; tenth and eleventh rows, double vandyke; twelfth row, single outline; thirteenth row, full diamond. The points in front began with six diamonds. The points on the sides began with five diamonds. For points in diamond stitch see Fig. 18, page 9.

Figure 39. English Smock. — In this play frock for a boy we show an English smock model. Every small boy would be well garbed in such a play garment as this comfortable and indestructible smock. The material was a stout Scotch madras, golden brown in color, with smocking of a different color; blue in this case. This garment, well buttoned up in front, the turn-over collar and cuffless sleeves with a bit of stitchery at the wrist, is as simple as one could possibly imagine. It is moderate in price, and looks

quite distinctive in the right place. The back of the garment shows smocking in the centre to match the smocking on the fronts. (See Fig. 52.)

Figures 40 and 41. — Figure 40 shows the detail of smock in the back. Figure 41 gives detail of the smocking on the fronts. The first row is diamond; second row, single cable; third row, diamond; fourth and fifth rows, single cable; sixth row, diamond; and the seventh row, wave in four stitches, worked so as to meet the row of diamond. The dotted transfer was used to mark up this piece of work and lines were wide apart as seen.

Figure 42. Ladies' Blouse of Checked Dimity. — Here we show a beautiful piece of work and a charming and useful garment. The material used was French dimity in a fine check, and the smocking threads were shaded from navy to very light, in five shades of blue, six-stranded cotton, two strands being

21

used for the smocking. The sleeves are elbow length, as shown, with smocking above a wide turned-up cuff. These cuffs and the collar have rolled hems, and then plain linen bands are added. Fagoting joins this linen edge or hem to the collar and cuffs. (See Fig. 21 page 10, for detail of this work.) The embroidered sprays, etc., are in outline stitch and bullion stitch. The curves are shaped, using a spool and pencil. The simulated buttons are made in a spider-web effect. (See Fig. 51, page 26, for detail.)

The preparation for these smocking stitches was done by taking up checks one-eighth of an inch apart and fifteen rows of shirs were required, as the entire shaded band at the finish in one-half diamond stitch is done free-hand without shirring; the folds simply held in place. When one has progressed as far as this waist, this free-hand work is natural, or ought to be. However, this very waist was the garment a pupil took as a first lesson; and this pupil excelled her teacher, too. The detail on page 22, Fig. 43, shows the work fully and gives an idea of the shading. Further explanation is entirely superfluous.

Figure 45.—This very pretty and stylish waist was designed and worked by a pupil as her first effort in smocking. The material was checked dimity, and the work was done using dark blue round thread cotton No. 20. The high collar is worn with a stock and turn-over of embroidery. The sleeves end in straight cuffs or bands with some bullion-stitch on them. The distinctive features of this waist are two: The white smocking at the neck above the blue smocking, and the tucks below the smocking. These tucks are edged with double over-and-over stitch and dotted with bullion stitches. The sleeves also show original treatment. Above the smocked band that is seen above the elbow are tucks again; thus undesirable fullness is eliminated. Attention to detail, combined with an artistic sense, made of a very inexpensive garment a thing of beauty. This waist opens under the side plait in front. The back is tucked and no color or smocking is used. The detail of work on the blouse is shown on page 22, Fig. 44.

The material, checked dimity, was smocked to the desired depth, as shown in white work above the blue band. The blue band, as shown by Fig. 44, was worked, the first row in single outline; the fourth and fifth rows in double vandyke; then single outline, and double cable and single outline followed with three rows of wave. Above this band the material is held in place, as shown, by rows in single cable stitch, worked with fine white cotton. This is a good idea and disposes of undesirable fullness in a novel manner. The fullness below the blue band is held by tucks that are ornamented and held in position by bullion stitch, which is another good idea. No sewing is done otherwise; in other words, the tucks are not held by a running stitch, as is usually the case.

Figure 46. Child's Princess Panel Frock.—This unusual model is made still more attractive by the use of smocking stitches in shaded effect. Blue was the color chosen for ornamenting this little frock for a girl of six years. The material was English checked dimity; turn-over collar, topped by a band of Irish crochet, ribbon run, holding in place the low Dutch neck. Embroidered scallops and bullion-stitched dots decorate the collar and cuffs, and the panel front also shows sprays of embroidery done in bullion stitch in shades of blue. The sleeves are finished with turn-over cuffs and some smocking is above the cuffs. The panel is finished with fagoting worked in two shades of blue between two rows of outline stitch; this fagoting extends around the waist of the dress to the back.

FIG. 43. DETAIL OF SMOCKING ON BLOUSE, FIG. 42

FIG. 44. DETAIL OF WAIST, FIG. 45

FIG. 45. WAIST OF CHECKED DIMITY WORKED IN DARK BLUE. See Fig. 44 and page 22

Figure 47 shows the detail of the smocking stitches on Child's Frock, Fig. 46. The elaborate effect is secured by the shading and the work being fine. However, it is extremely simple, as only three or four different stitches are used, viz.: the first line is in single outline; the second line in double cable; the third line, single outline; the fourth, fifth, and sixth lines are used for the double vandyke; and the seventh line shows single outline again. From the eighth line is worked twelve rows of wave, using three stitches rather close together and shaded from dark to light. (See the illustration.) These lines of wave are worked without preparation, work simply being held in place.

Figure 48. Child's Frock.—This little frock shows pink shades in the smocking stitches and bullion embroidery is used to further decorate the garment. This embroidery lends itself especially well where smocking is done. Cross stitch also is very appropriate and much used in little floral designs. Pretty linen dresses and play frocks are shown in colors, embroidered with birds and animals in lovely colors on the collar and cuffs. These are very un-

23

usual, and high class when the embroidery is done in cross stitch or Kensington stitch. Our little frock has three-and-one-half-inch tucks worked in of stitches and the quality of the work, as well as coloring combined to make this a very pretty frock, and well worth the task of making.

FIG. 46. CHILD'S PRINCESS PANEL FROCK OF DIMITY

SMOCKED AND EMBROIDERED IN SHADES OF BLUE. See page 22

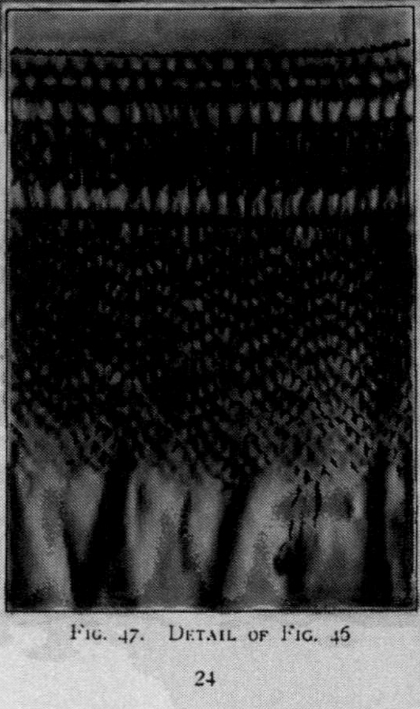

FIG. 47. DETAIL OF FIG. 46

outline stitch in shades as shown. The material is fine handkerchief linen. Two and one-half yards are required. The sleeves show tucking and it serves to subdue the fullness, as well as adding to the appearance. A four-inch hem, a bit of ribbon and one yard of Valenciennes lace, and some Irish insertion finish the frock. (See Fig. 49.)

Figure 49 gives the detail of the work on Fig. 48. The stitched method was used for preparing for the work, ten rows being required. As the points were free-hand, the arrangement

Figure 50. Garden Smock.— Leaving frocks for a time, we show in this illustration one of the garden smocks so much in favor. The usefulness and comfort embodied in this model are well known, and from a modest beginning these smocks have grown in favor until now some of them are sumptuous affairs. When such materials as Italian silks and pussy willow silks, also crêpe de Chine are employed, these smocks are delightful. Among materials a silk and cotton, and silk and wool crêpe, are favorites and also moderate in price. Take one of these crêpes in white, smock it in a favorite color, put on a

24

striped collar and cuffs in silk to match the s m o c k i n g stitches and a plain white sash, one has a most distinctive garment; and it launders, too. A white Italian silk had pale lemon smocking, with just a touch of green and black stitchery. A collar and cuffs showed stitches in these colors. The sash of the Italian silk, with the ends crossstitched a bit in the same colors was charming.

The model shown was developed in coral pink crêpe; the collar, cuffs, and belt were in white crêpe; all the stitches were worked in colors, shades of pink, some black and white. The garment was laced in front in true smock fashion. White crêpe buttons over ivory m o l d s w e r e worked in spider effect in shades of pink. (See Fig. 51.) Figure 52 gives the detail of the stitches used on the belt, collar and cuffs, consisting of an outline in

Fig. 48. Another Model for a Child's Frock. See detail, Fig. 49, and page 23

Fig. 49. Detail of Fig. 48

b l a c k a n d b u t t o n h o l e - s t i t c h e s in two shades of pink on either s i d e. T h e w o r k is all e a s y to do and fascinating to a degree.

This g a r m e n t has a yoke to which t h e smocked fronts are attached. The back is in one piece with smocking

midway between the shoulders to match that on the fronts. The illustration shows an effective combination of the different colors.

We read of smocks and smocking in Queen Anne's time and earlier, and a description of garments smocked in golden threads and in silver on silk and satin has an attractive sound. With each revival of a mode progress is made, and in embroidered smocking this era has made an important advance. Besides, embroidered smocking is purely American, and now one can smock anything and in any grade, as fine as possible or the reverse.

Figure 53. Sports Smock.—This sports smock was developed in blue crêpe cloth with crêpe for collar, cuffs, and belt. A row of outlining in heavy silk and double over-and-over stitch is the decoration on the collar, cuffs, and belt. Buttons with embroidery are seen on the fronts and on the belt. The

tion of simple stitches used on the Child's Party Frock, Fig. 56. The upper part of the design is worked around the skirt. The lower part of the design is on the top and bottom of the waist front. The work on the sleeves is the same as on the skirt. Eight lines were stitched for the skirt. On the first line was worked double cable; on the second, third, and fourth lines is worked the wave, using four stitches up and four down; the fifth line, double cable. The point is worked in diamond, two stitches up and two stitches down, worked across the line, then divided into uneven numbers. Make the points in even numbers, leaving one diamond between each point. The smocking on the waist consists of — first line, double cable; second line, dots; third, double cable; work fourth, fifth, and sixth lines wave in four stitches without preparation. Figure 55 shows the smocking stitches in detail. This is extremely simple work, and the coloring, shades of rose, is very good. The dimity also is of the best, and the lace at the neck and sleeves gives an additional finish to a very pretty frock for a four - year - old. The simulated buttons are in the now familiar spid-

FIG. 52. DETAIL OF STITCH USED IN FIG. 39. See page 25

FIG. 50. SPORTS SMOCK OF CORAL PINK EMBROIDERED IN SHADES OF PINK, BLACK, AND WHITE. See page 24

smocking is done in white. (See Fig. 54.)

Figure 54.—This illustration shows the detail of the smocking stitches used on Fig. 53. Twenty-one rows were stitched on the sewing-machine for lines and spaces. Seven stitches to the inch were used. After the usual preparation, smocking stitches were worked as follows: First row, single outline; second row, two double cable and one full diamond across the line; third row, single outline. Three rows of wave, using three stitches up and three stitches down follow, and then on the eighth line we work cable stitch across five times, forming the band. A band in feathered diamond, of six rows or five full diamonds, comes next, followed by a band of cable, as in the beginning of the pattern; single outline, double cable and diamond and single outline finish the design.

Figure 55. — This detail shows the combina-

er's web. Indeed they are used on sleeves, at neck and in the back, for this frock is the same in work back and front. The sleeves are laid in tucks, doing away with unnecessary fullness. Cords and tassels are of the same cotton as used for the smocking stitches. This model has been much admired, and looks very simple when worn. It is a pretty party or dancing school frock for a small maiden. The frontispiece

FIG. 51. BUTTON WORKED IN SPIDER WEB

26

Fig. 53. Sports Smock of Blue Crêpe with White Collar, Cuffs, and Belt. See detail, Fig. 54, and page 25

shows another pretty adaptation of this simple smocking design on a child's party frock.

Three shades of a color are recommended for this pattern, either rose or blue, as preferred, and two or three threads of stranded cotton are best adapted for working. Use the darker shade for the lines of wave-stitch, the next shade for the double cable stitch on either side and, commencing with the darkest, use all three shades for the points in diamond stitch, ending with the lightest shade at the tips. The clusters of bullion stitch which finish the tips of the diamond-stitch points should be in the darkest shade.

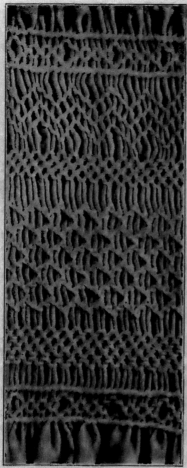

FIG. 54. DETAIL OF SMOCKING, FIG. 53

skirt and the under-arm seams are covered with the same fancy stitch.

Figure 56. Child's Party Dress.—(See Fig. 55.) The material selected for this little frock was fine-quality English dimity, with a stripe of three cords, the plain space being equal in width to the corded lines. There are six corded lines to the inch, and these cords or corded lines were used in shirring for the smocking, taking each line for one stitch and omitting the plain spaces. To secure straight and even spaces for these shirring lines the sewing-machine was used—an application of the stitched method mentioned many times in the descriptions of work in this book. All that this or similar cases demand is straight lines to guide the shirring. A long loose stitch can be used on the machine.

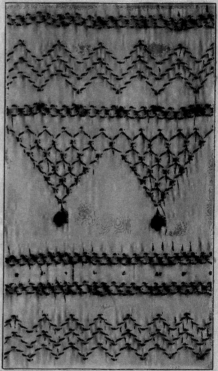

FIG. 55. DETAIL OF STITCHES. DOUBLE CABLE, WAVE, AND DIAMOND AS USED ON FIG. 56. See page 29

Mention has been made of the simulated buttons in spider-web stitch. The bars are worked directly into the material, and the spider-web then woven on the bars is illustrated on page 26, Fig. 51. Use the darkest shade for the bars and the lightest for weaving.

This is a particularly pretty model for the small child, and any simple cutting pattern may be used which has set-in sleeves and an attached gathered or plaited skirt, allowing for the extra fullness of material required for smocking, as described in the introductory chapters to this book. If a wide hem is allowed, the skirt can be easily lengthened to accommodate the growing child.

Neck and sleeve edges are finished with bands of the fagoting stitch, illustrated on page 10, outlined on both edges with a darker shade. The joining of waist and

Figure 57.—In this illustration we have a new feature; indeed, two new features,—the double diamond wave and buttonhole stitch. The piece is worked on madras and stitched lines and spaces were used for preparation. Sixteen lines were stitched, using seven stitches to the inch. Work was drawn up, pulled into place, and smocking commenced on the first line in single outline; on the second line, single buttonhole

28

stitch; on the third line, single cable stitch; on the fourth line, diamond stitch, using two stitches down to the fifth line and up to the fourth line, down to the fifth line and so on across the work. On the sixth line diamond stitch is worked up to the fifth line, down to the sixth line, up to the fifth line, forming a full diamond. Three more rows of diamond stitch are worked in the same manner, forming a band in diamond. On the ninth line is worked a row of single cable. The double diamond wave consists of

manner, keeping the points directly in line with those of the small diamond wave and meeting it at every other point. This gives one-half of a double diamond pattern. The second half of the double diamond is worked the same as the first half, except that it is reversed. The buttonhole stitch on the second line is the same as used in embroidery.

Figure 58.—A honeycomb diamond used in connection with a band or other stitchery is somewhat out of

FIG. 56. CHILD'S PARTY DRESS OF STRIPED DIMITY SMOCKED IN SHADES OF ROSE. See Fig. 55 and page 28

one row of diamond wave outlined top and bottom by a row of stitches twice the number used for the small diamond, joining the small diamond on every second point as shown. It is best to work the small diamond first, leaving spaces above and below for the large diamond, or upper and lower lines shown. Note the illustration carefully. Work from the thirteenth line to the twelfth, using three stitches, down to the thirteenth, and so on across. For the outer row of wave commence on the twelfth line and work to the second line above (tenth) and down again in same

the ordinary in appearance. It looks attractive, and is desirable where a small or fine honeycomb pattern can be used. Such a pattern furnishes the often-needed finish for a piece of work in honeycomb stitch. This illustration was prepared, using the sewing-machine for lines and spaces, and the stitch was worked from right to left.

Now, honeycomb stitch can be worked in several ways. It is the only smocking stitch so adaptable. The various illustrations in this book fully illustrate this principle. (See Figs. 29 and 30 on page 14, Fig. 32

on page 15, where the work was prepared and worked, using the tucked method — *these* examples being worked from left to right.) When using the dot or transfer method, the work can be done working from

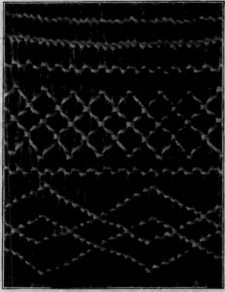

FIG. 57. A GOOD SMOCKING PATTERN, SHOWING TWO NEW FEATURES, DOUBLE DIAMOND WAVE AND BUTTONHOLE STITCH. See page 28

either left or right, but the diamond is best secured with two stitches over, worked from right to left, as in the case of the dot used by embroiderers. Circumstances govern the method used for working the honeycomb stitch. The material may be gathered, and the stitch taken on the folds, or the stitch worked on the dots without the preliminary gathering.

In working from left to right, using the dot or transfer method, the progress is slow, and the work is not well secured, although leaving a cleaner piece of work on the wrong side. However, the right side of smocking is the side that interests most workers.

The band commencing this design has been described several times, and we refer to page 8, Fig. 17. It consists of one row in outline, one row in double cable and single diamond in combination; then outline again. Fourteen rows in all were stitched and shirred in the usual manner for this design. Using this method, the needle carrying the shirring-thread is put into the holes made by the machine-needle. In the succeeding rows the folds or plaits so secured are exactly followed, the lines marked by the sewing-machine being the width of the presser-foot apart.

Begin the honeycomb band on the fourth row at the right end of the work. Secure the thread on the first plait on the wrong side, bringing the needle up to the right side through the second plait. Take the first and second plaits together with two stitches over, as when

working an embroidered dot. Then from the wrong side come down to the second line; bring your needle through the third plait. Take the third and second plaits together twice as before. Then from the wrong side again pass up to the first line. Take the fourth and third plaits together twice and proceed across the line. The second row is worked from the third line to the second line, forming a diamond. Do not draw your thread too tight in passing from stitch to stitch, as it detracts from the elasticity of the work.

Figure 59. Apron. — An apron smocked is not so new as pretty, and this one is of unusual excellence, as it is provided with three capacious pockets. This apron is obviously intended for a sewing-apron. The material required is one and one-half yards, one yard wide. Dimity was used in this case. The strings and added hems were cut crosswise on the goods. Usually this is not a good plan to follow, but in this case it was done. The pockets are simply turned up and feather-stitched to make the divisions. Feather-stitching is used on all edges, to hold the hems, etc., in place. The sprays are in outline and in bullion stitch, Fig. 23. The smocking was done on lines secured by taking up the checks every other one. Eight rows were used. The points were done freehand. The smocking pattern is clearly shown in Fig. 58. The apron shows a small bib decorated in keeping with the balance of the apron. Straps or bretelles can be used in place of the bib, if desired, and similarly decorated.

The apron shown is extremely attractive when taffeta silk is the material selected, and, of course, silks used for the smocking stitches. Rose-colored stranded cottons were used in the case of the apron shown, and two threads at one time. Any smocking pattern pre-

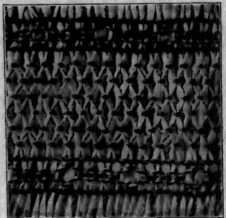

FIG. 58. HONEYCOMB SMOCKING IN COMBINATION WITH SIMPLE STITCHES. See page 28

ferred can be used, and many forms of embroidery stitches also are properly used.

Figure 60. — The first row is single outline; second row, single outline; third row, single outline; one-half diamond is worked between the first and second and second and third lines. The curved wave, worked in outline stitch (Fig. 19, page 9), occupies a space of five lines; working four stitches up with the thread below the needle, three stitches across the line, thread below the needle; four stitches down, with the thread above the needle, and three stitches on the line with the thread above the needle; then four stitches up to the fourth line and three stitches across the line as before. Next row is worked in the same manner from the line below, and dots are placed in the centre, working from the right hand. The sixth and seventh lines are single outline with one-half diamond worked in the space between the two lines. One row of full diamond is worked below this, as the preparation for the point. These diamonds are divided into unequal numbers; for instance, they are divided into five diamonds, and the point is commenced four diamonds, as the space of one diamond is always left between the points after the first row is worked. (See illustration.) Any number of diamonds can begin a point, that can be suitably spaced.

In working the points on this apron, it is a good plan to work from each end, putting any uneven spaces in the centre point, which may contain one or two diamonds more than the others. Count off your diamonds and spaces in the first row, and be governed by what you have. There is no arbitrary law about these things. The worker can use her judgment in the matter, making the points large or small.

Frontispiece (page 2). — This illustration shows how charming the little smocked

FIG. 50. APRON WITH POCKETS. See detail Fig. 60, and page 30

FIG. 60. DETAIL OF FIG. 59

frocks are for children. On this garment smocking is used only to secure the fullness at the top of the skirt and on the sleeves. The waist portion is embroidered in the same color as the smocking, and Irish crochet lace is used for neck finish and heading at the waist line. The edges of sleeves and the frills on the waist are finished with the reverse over-and-over stitch (Fig. 24, page 11), also in color.

The smocking pattern is very similar to that shown in detail by Fig. 55, page 28.

Laundering Smocking.—Use a good soap, Ivory preferred. Wash by hand quickly, rinse thoroughly, and do not starch the smocking. Let the garment hang in the air long enough to partly dry; roll it in a clean cloth and let it remain for about one hour; then iron as usual, only do not iron your smocking. Gently pull it into its original position. After all this is done the smocked portions of the garment can be placed right side up over a Turkish towel, folded several times and lightly touched with a warm iron. When the smocking is finished, it can be held over an inverted iron with the wrong side of the smocking to the iron, as in steaming velvet; this stiffens the plaits. It is never advisable to boil or scald a garment that is worked in colors.

Pattern for the Transfer Dot Method of Marking for Shirring
Threads as described on Page 5

PREPARE a working pattern by placing thin paper over pattern of dots below, marking dots with pencil, and transfer to material by means of carbon paper placed face down between working pattern and material, using a pencil or any blunt-pointed instrument. The working pattern may be made any length or depth desired by moving the paper along, using the last row of dots as a key to keep the subsequent rows even.

The points at the bottom are of use chiefly in Honeycomb Smocking. (See page 17.) In making additional points, repeat from two vertical centre lines of dots in middle point as many times as desired.

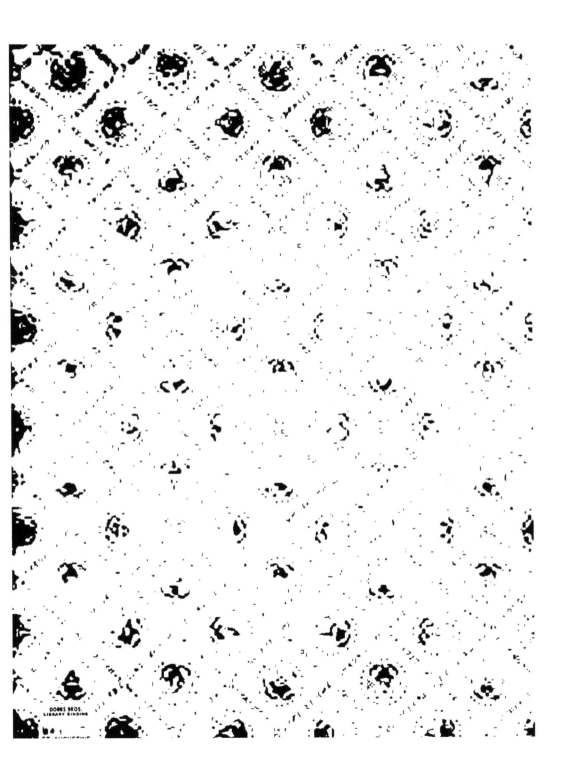

Milton Keynes UK
Ingram Content Group UK Ltd.
UKHW022119210923
429156UK00005B/95

9 781015 455641